Louis Weiss

More Light

A Rational Treatise on Biblical Subjects

Louis Weiss

More Light
A Rational Treatise on Biblical Subjects

ISBN/EAN: 9783337254810

Printed in Europe, USA, Canada, Australia, Japan

Cover: Foto ©Lupo / pixelio.de

More available books at **www.hansebooks.com**

MORE LIGHT.

A RATIONAL TREATISE ON

BIBLICAL SUBJECTS,

BY

RABBI L. WEISS,

COLUMBUS, GA.

THE BLOCH PUBLISHING AND PRINTING COMPANY,
CINCINNATI, 1892.

PREFACE.

"Seize upon truth wherever found,
On Christian or on heathen ground;
Among your friends, among your foes;—
The plant's divine where'er it grows."

With this principle imbedded in my breast do I enter the task of shedding *more light* on subjects that so often come before us inquiringly.

It is not my object to nullify my neighbor's creed and religion and establish my own, but to pave the path that leads us nearer to one another.

"MORE LIGHT!" were Goethe's last words, and just as the human eye delights in light so should the human soul be inspired with more light.

May, then, the reader that had gained the light of religion, in a measure that illuminates the narrow sphere of dogmatic sectarianism only, glean *more light* from this little volume—light that illumines the entire universe—and recognize the Fatherhood of God and brotherhood of man.

THE AUTHOR.

WHAT SHALL WE DO TO BE SAVED?

THIS question is foreign to Jews and Judaism. It was never propounded to or by Moses, the Prophets, or any Jewish writer of Biblical or Talmudical literature. It is a New Testament inquiry, which later became misconstrued and is by many misunderstood, which I will demonstrate in my next chapter. At present I will merely show why this question is not agitated by Jews and Jewish writers. Rabbis that have lived long before us have agreed that צדיקים שבאומות העולם יש להם חלק לעולם הבא "the righteous, of whatever people, have a share in the world hereafter," without laying down a rule for *non-Jews* how to be righteous.

Some Christians say, to be righteous one must believe in Christ; but Jews and Judaism do not deprive any one of his rights to think and to exercise his virtue according to the dictates of his belief. It matters not what the ceremonies appertaining to his worship are as long as his propensities otherwise are beneficial to the world and mankind. לא המדרש עיקר אלא המעשה "Not the creed, but the deed, is the cardinal principle" in Judaism; and it is proper to say here that if virtue and morality are the saving propensities of man, we can draw no line of separation between the saved ones, for these attributes are innate with all enlightened people without regard of creed.

Let it further be understood that there is no *Jewish* virtue or morality, nor *Christian* virtue and morality. *Virtue* is virtue, and *morality* is morality, regardless of whose breast they abide in. "What makes me a good Jew makes you a good Christian," said Lessing, and it is God's truth.

The dime of the charitable Christian will not buy for the poor, hungry person a larger loaf of bread than will the dime of the charitable Jew.

The chastity that makes a Christian woman pure and virtuous makes not less so the Jewish woman.

Purity is purity, and morality is morality, with everybody.

> "Shall ignorance of good and ill
> Dare to direct th' eternal will?
> Seek virtue; and of that possess'd,
> To Providence resign the rest."

Enlightenment, then, tells us that God *gave not* religion for His own edification — for we can not add to His glory, nor can we magnify His greatness. He gave religion to edify mankind, to perfect *man's* morals, and to make *man* virtuous and righteous. If, then, my neighbor's religion has the efficacy to do that for him, and mine is as efficacious with me, the just and truthful God will assuredly not disregard the good qualities of man because his ceremonies are not conformable to a certain church ritual.

Ceremonials are intended to evoke solemnity and devotion, but are otherwise of no vital importance, and not necessarily essential, and those who believe that it is necessary to believe in Jesus as a Christ, in Mohammed as a Redeemer, or in Moses as a Mediator between God and man, impeach the loving kindness and justness of God. Man would not reject his child, and especially a good child, merely because of the opinion it entertains, thinking it does so to please its father, but God is supposed to send the best man, the purest woman and the most righteous person to perdition for the mere fault of not believing in Christ as a Savior—a faith they *can not* comprehend, hence can not accept.

Scriptures tell us of Absalom (II. Samuel xix.), the son of David, how perniciously he revolted against his own father, who loved him with fond devotion, and when he met with a horrible death when on his way to persecute and oppress his father, the father wept bitterly and lamented over his son. So could we to-day find parents that would clasp to their bosom their child, even though it were the most perverse and degraded of creatures, especially if it would come suppliantly before them; but God, who can see the petitioner's real sincerity and contrition, who can perceive that the soul is truly repentant—as all secrets and hidden things are revealed to Him—is less merciful than man. He will not receive the sinner, nor the righteous, except they come to Him through a savior. Is this rational? Judaism says, no! "The Lord is good to all, and His mercy extends to all His creatures" (Ps. cxlv. 9), and the question, "What shall we do to be saved?" remains forever inapt to embody in its precepts.

When Moses gave the laws to Israel—laws that became the groundwork of all laws and creeds—he gave them בהם וחי "TO LIVE BY THEM." (See Lev. xviii. 18.) In his last premonitions and admonitions (Deutr. xxx. 19) he lays before Israel life and death, blessing and curse, but " *Choose thou life!* " said he, " *that thou shalt live* and *also thy children.* " Here would have been the time to impress them with a soul-saving doctrine by a savior, instead of which this greatest of teachers impresses his flock before he dies with the all-important and sublime doctrine that teaches LIFE.

Thus Judaism does not agitate the question, "How shall we be saved in the hereafter?" but it particularly teaches us how to live here. Real life on earth will secure us, unconsciously, life everlasting, and if one should ask us for a substitute for the question before us we would ask one more important and more sublime, viz.: " *How shall we live? and how shall we impart life to our children?* "

WHAT MUST I DO TO BE SAVED ?

THAT the soul-saving theory as conceived and construed by Christians is not concurred in by Jews and Judaism, I have demonstrated in the preceding chapter; and now I intend to show that the New Testament itself does not promulgate the idea, but later commentators must have adopted it.

That Jews do not accept the authenticity of the New Testament is hardly necessary to mention as a defense why they do not accept doctrines prescribed therein, but were they inclined to accept this particular doctrine that so deeply concerns the soul, they would be at a loss to find it

promulgated in its pages. It appears but once in the entire
book, where a prison-keeper asks Paul and Silas, "Sirs,
what must I do to be saved?" (Acts xvi. 30), to which the
answer, of course is, "Believe in Jesus." But what was
meant by being saved? That will now be my object of
demonstration. With Israelites it signified nothing else but
temporal salvation, and so it was spoken of by Scriptural
writers, and also later by the rabbins, who, when they agitated
the salvation of the soul, spoke of it in unequivocal terms
as הבא עולם חיי "*the life of the hereafter*," or "*eternal life*."
To be saved, therefore, and to inherit eternal life were two
different expectations as implanted in the breast of Israel.
One evoked hope of temporal or material existence, the
other of celestial or eternal existence.

We read in Scriptures (Judges iii. 9) that "the Lord
raised up a *savior* to Israel"—in the person of Othniel, who
saved them from calamity and disaster. In II. Kings
(xiii. 5) we read that "the Lord gave Israel a *savior*"— in
the person of Jehoahaz.

Nehemiah (ix. 27) says: "Thou (God) gavest them (Israel) *saviors* that saved them," etc.

It is not necessary to sift the entire Scriptures. This is
sufficient to substantiate the assertion that Israel and Scripture writers understood in the term to be saved temporal
salvation, and the savior was a human being that led them
on to this salvation; while the salvation theory as promulgated by Christians is contradictory of the manifold assurances enunciated in Scriptures, that *God alone, and none
else*, is the savior of Israel and also of all mankind.

I will cite a few of the many assurances:

"I am the Lord; beside me there is no savior." (Isaiah
xliii. 11.)

"A just God and a savior there is none beside me." (Ibid. xlv. 21.)

"All flesh shall know that I am thy savior," etc. (Ibid. xlix. 26.)

"Thou shalt know that I am thy savior," etc. (Ibid. lx. 16.)

" There is no savior beside me." (Hosea xiii. 4)

The most striking proof that God is the savior of all mankind indiscriminately, and extending His salvation unconditionally (and without vicarious atonement) is found in Isaiah (xlv. 22, 23), " Look (or turn) unto me, and be ye saved, *all the ends of the earth*, for I am God and none else. I have *sworn* by *myself*, the word is gone out of my mouth in righteousness, and *shall not* return." Did God become a perjurer? We believe not.

That Israel believed to find in virtue and morality the redeeming qualities of that salvation which the word bears on its surface, and as demonstrated here, is clearly evident when we read Jeremiah iv. 14. He says :

" Wash thy heart that thou mayest be saved." The prophet does not urge us to believe, to pray, to be baptized, or to conform to any prescribed ceremony, but exhorts us to purify the heart in order to be saved.

Now, we ask, who wrote the New Testament? Jews, of course, with Jewish thoughts, Jewish sentiments and Jewish tenets pervading their breasts, and their writings bear no marks of any difference as regards the precepts and principles of the Jewish writers of previous ages, and when they wrote of the saving of the soul they expressed it, like other Jews, with *eternal life*.

When Jesus was asked (Matt. xix. 16; Mark x. 17; Luke xviii. 17), " What shall I do that I may inherit *eternal life?* "

(not to be saved) he did not reply, "Believe in me," but he said, " Follow the Commandments." To inherit eternal life faith was not a sufficient attribute; the deed, and not the creed, secures, according to extant Jewish doctrines, eternal life, and Jesus the Jew taught it not different.

At another time (Luke x. 25) he answered the same question with " Love the Lord with all thy heart, and with all thy soul, and with all thy might (vide Deuter. vi. 5), and love thy neighbor as thyself " (vide Lev. xix. 18). This alone would suffice to prove that the New Testament writers did not confound the theory of temporal salvation with that of eternal life. But we will quote one more instance of striking evidence :

When Jesus healed a sick woman (Luke vii. 50), and another time a blind man (Ibid. xviii. 42), he said to each, " Thy faith hath saved thee." Saved from what? From sickness, and brought to health. It could not have meant that their souls were saved, as they were yet alive; and however pure in faith they may have been at that time, they could yet have lost all faith before they died; hence it is clearly evident that Jesus alluded to their temporal salvation — they were saved from malady and brought to health.

When the disciples of the Nazarene reformer taught to believe in Jesus and be saved, they promulgated a doctrine for publicans, sinners and degraded heathens who had no divine religion to prompt them to lead a better life ; but the Jews had sublime precepts and beautiful doctrines, and to be good and righteous they had only to follow them. But those of the new creed tried to save — that is, to a loftier existence — people that would not listen to Jewish doctrines, hence the best way to teach them was to believe in their leader and master, to follow his ways, precepts and example. With the rise and progress of that Christianity, which introduced measures of diametrical difference between the religion of Israel and its own, which is incontrovertibly of a later period by more than three hundred years than the life and existence of Jesus, rose and progressed the idea that modern divines and commentators entertain regarding salvation of the soul. Their idea, however, rests on blind faith, unsupported by reason, and misconstrued from Scripture passages, contradictory of their own *golden rule* to " do unto others as they would be done by." They would not like to be damned, but they damn others who conform not to their faith. They want their opinion to be respected, but the opinion of others who do not believe as they do they consider wrong; otherwise they would have no damnatory doctrines.

What must I do to be saved? then, should be answered thus: Endeavor to be a good and upright man or woman, no matter what your creed is. Be honest, be just in all your ways and dealings, and never do to others that which would displease you if others did it to you.

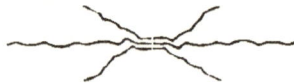

DID THE JEWS REJECT CHRIST?

THE imputation of Christians is that the Jews rejected Christ, but, although it would be sufficiently reasonable to reply that the Jews never expected a Messiah of such character as Christians made of Jesus, viz., a divine being, yet I will not enlarge on that argument, but look into the pages of the New Testament and see how this imputation is substantiated.

Of all the New Testament writers John alone says (John i. 11): "He came unto his own, but his own received him not." Matthew, Mark and Luke merely chronicle the words of Jesus: "The stone which the builders rejected has become the chief of the corner," which is a verbatim quotation from Psalm cxviii. 22, but they say nothing as to who were meant by the builders; and if they said plainly, as did John, that it meant the Jews, we would still investigate the whole writings, even as we do now, and come to conclusions accordingly.

We read (Matt. xxii. 37; Mark xii. 30; Luke x. 27, that Jesus was teaching, "Thou shalt love the Lord thy God with all thy heart and with all thy soul," etc., "and thou shalt love thy neighbor as thyself."

Was there in this anything for Jews to accept? Have they not had this in their own Scriptures (*vide* Deuter. vi. 5, and Levit. xix. 8), written and commended by Moses nigh two thousand years before?

Jesus taught: "What you would that man should do to you, so shall you do to him." Did not the Jews hear the meek and gentle Hillel giving this precept to a heathen who wanted to embrace Judaism, in words very little different, yet meaning the same, viz., "What is displeasing to thee do it not to others?"

To an inquirer who wanted to know what he should do to inherit eternal life, Jesus said : "If thou wilt enter eternal life, keep the Commandments." (Matt. xix. 17.) Surely there was nothing new in this for Jews, upon whom the Commandments were made obligatory on Sinai by God's own revelation.

To the question, which was the first Commandment, Jesus replied (Mark xii. 28) : "Hear, O Israel! the Lord our God is one!" This beautiful confession of God's indivisible unity was then, as it is to-day, embodied in every prayer of the Israelites — prayers private and public, composed for both reformers and orthodox. So in this, like in all other teachings of Jesus of an ethical and divine character, the Jews could not discover anything that they had not previously heard and accepted.

It is now meet to ask the question, did he ever offer himself to the Jews for acceptence?

Let us see. We read (Matt. iv. 23) that he went about all Galilee teaching and preaching in the Synagogues. What he preached and what he taught is not specified, nor was he rejected anywhere, hence we can infer from this that he must have preached and taught that which was compatible with Judaism. He was, however, a reformer, and to propagate his ideas he gave the Jews the assurance (*vide* Matt. v 17) : "Think not that I came to destroy the law and the prophets. I came not to destroy, but to fulfill." Like the aim of all Jewish reformers, to do away with rabbinism and priest-ocracy and strengthen the tenets prescribed in Scriptures, such must have been the aim of Jesus, and he manifested it in all his manners and utterances.

When the Pharisees on one occasion saw him feasting with a common class of people and they asked his disciples, "Why eateth your master with publicans and sinners?" he replied, "The whole need no physician, but the sick. I came not to call the righteous, but sinners, to repentance." (Matt. ix. 11-13.) Does this not plainly indicate that he considered the Pharisees righteous, not needing his ministration, and consequently went to call publicans and sinners to a better and purer life? If he afterward did speak harshly to some scribes and Pharisees, that does not signify that all scribes and Pharisees, and all Jews especially, were included in his condemnatories. The ones he spoke to first must have been different from those he spoke to afterward; all were not wicked, nor did he say that they were.

We find him (Ibid. lx. 6) charging his disciples to go to the *lost* sheep of Israel, not to *Israel* the *lost* sheep, not to the whole nation, but to those that were *lost* to the nation. He himself, however, did not go; he only sent his disciples; but they did not go that time, nor is it stated why.

How tolerant the Jews were appears from the story chronicled in John viii. 7, where they brought before him an adulterous woman, asking him to pass judgment upon her' and he passed this sentence: "He who is without sin among you let him first cast a stone at her." And immediately, one by one, they left the room, leaving him alone with the woman.

This demonstrates with what tolerance Jesus was treated, when they submitted a case for trial to him which belonged to local and regularly installed judges; and, furthermore, when sentence was passed — perhaps beyond what they expected — they silently withdrew, leaving the case without any further prosecution. Does this show any signs of rejection of Jesus?

Furthermore, it is meet to ask, why was the New Testament written in Greek and not in Hebrew if it was at all intended for a Hebrew people?

That Greek was then the language of the country, we are well aware, but the Jews could best speak the Hebrew language, and that was the language they all spoke; while the Greek language may have been spoken well by some, it was not spoken well by others, and very imperfectly by the masses; and besides their Scriptures were in Hebrew, their divine services were conducted in Hebrew, even more so than they are to-day, and Jesus himself spoke Hebrew in preference to the Greek, which is evident from the last words he spoke on the cross: " *Eli, eli, lamah Shabaktain?*" (Matt. xvii. 46.)

This suffices to show that there was nothing in the teachings of Jesus to indicate that he offered to the Jews a new creed, nor that he anywhere offered himself to them as their messiah. His aims, from all appearances, were to impart some of the moral ethics of the Jews to the Gentiles, who had no divine religion, and who would not go the Jews to receive it. Jesus lived and died as a Jew. He took pains during his lifetime to observe the feasts of the Jews, he advocated their moral laws, and words from their Scriptures closed his lips in death. In short, a Christ was neither offered to nor rejected by the Jews; nor was the book that teaches Christianity intended for Jews.

DID THE JEWS CRUCIFY CHRIST?

THIS would hardly need a reply from the Jews, for even if it were indisputably evident that the Jews at that remote time did crucify Jesus of Nazareth, their posterity could not reasonably be held accountable for wrongs committed over eighteen hundred years ago. Yet for the sake of truth we will examine into this matter. Before investigating, however, whether Jews did crucify Jews, we will ask, are we still held accountable for the deed?

Matthew chronicles (xxvii. 25), which is corroborated by none of the other Gospel writers: "His (Jesus') blood be on us and our children." But God, who, according to Scripture, would visit* the iniquities of the fathers upon their children unto the *third* and *fourth* generation (*vide* Exod. xx. 5; Deuter. v. 9), would not accept such pledge. He would not listen to such a heartless avowal and permit it to stand forever.

Man would not be so merciless as to mete out punishment to innocent people merely because their parents vowed so, much less an omniscient Father. However reasonable this sounds, yet some will say that the ways of the Lord are unsearchable, and man's argument, however forcible it may be, will not be regarded worthy of consideration unless it is supported by Biblical statements; and to answer it thus it it is meet that we begin with the descendants and progeny of the Jews.

---

*Explanatory of this see on another page the subject, "Will God punish children for the sins of parents?"

According to Scriptures, the lineage of the Jews is traced back to Shem, who manifested toward his father filial love and respect, of which his brothers Ham and Japhet were void (*vide* Gen. ix. 23); hence writers determined that he was more refined and had naturally better blood in his veins, which was transmitted into the veins of his descendants. Thus we find that his descendants, Abraham, Isaac and Jacob, are chosen by God, in preference to other people around them, to become the standard-bearers of God's truth, and this distinction was ingrafted into their posterity, Israel; the blood of Shem ran in the veins of these patriarchs, and their blood ran and still runs in the veins of their descendants.

Notwithstanding that the Jews descended from an idolatrous people — all were idolators at one time — there is no people and there never was a people who could claim a purer progeny, which is evident from the fact that into their hands was intrusted the transcendent glory of light divine.

Long, long before other people had conceived the remotest idea of a God the Jews worshiped the true God; and the law which they received on Sinai, prohibiting debasing and fallacious idolatries, making filial respect obligatory, and forbidding murder, adultery and theft — crimes that have cursed and blasted the social and moral life of all other nations — could only improve their virtues and attributes. And it is a fact beyond dispute that theirs was the only code of all ancient laws that contained the element of perpetuity.

Whenever they violated or disregarded these laws it was always due to a lack of good government, for no sooner had a leader risen among them than they awoke to consciousness of their error and amended their ways.

Time and ages have made many a change in the Jews, but they have by no means degenerated or retrograded; on the contrary, they have improved, progressed and advanced, and at the time when the Nazarene reformer existed in Jerusalem, they were, if not better, assuredly not worse, than formerly.

There may have been — nay, there were — some wicked ones among them, who caused and created disunion and discord among the people; but *all* of a nation are never corrupt; *all* of a race, creed or sect are not nefarious sinners; hence when the New Testament writers chronicle that the cry was made, "Crucify him! crucify him!" we must protest and say that these writers must either have made false statements or made a mistake themselves — mistaking the Romans for Jews.

In vain it may be claimed that the Bible was written by inspiration, and that its pages are free from mistakes, for both the Old and New Testaments contain mistakes, and merely to justify my assertion I will quote from Matthew xxvii. 9, where it says: "Then was fulfilled that which was spoken by Jeremiah, the prophet, saying, 'And they took the thirty pieces of silver,'" etc. This is not found in Jeremiah. Is this, then, not a mistake? Again it says (ibid. 35): "And they crucified him and parted his garments, casting lots, that it might be fulfilled which was spoken by the prophet: They parted my garments among them, and upon my vestures did they cast lots." By which prophet was this spoken? By none. Is this not a mistake? And if these are mistakes they are enough to indicate that there may be still more mistakes, among which is this particular one we write of.

If the New Testament had stated that Jesus suffered death by the impeachment of the Jews, notwithstanding that the Jews had at that time neither power nor influence with the Government, we could still infer that he died, if not by the hands, yet through the instrumentality of the Jews; but the statement alone that he was crucified is evidence that the Jews had nothing to do with it; for according to Jewish law punishment of death was meted out by stoning, burning, beheading or strangulation (hanging.) Crucifying even a guilty man would have been as sinful as to kill an innocent man, and the whole Jewry would not have tolerated this, if it was in their power, and if it was not in their power, they certainly could not have effected the crucifixion. If the Jews had had so much influence as to put Jesus to death, they could have also obtained privilege to do it according to their own law; the crucifixion, however, shows that they were void of all and any power and influence.

Another evidence that the story of the crucifixion is incorrect we find in the statement that he was crucified on the sixth day of the week, Friday; for not only would the Jews not have executed a man on Passover, nor have been present at the crucifixion, but the first day of Passover, according to our almanac system, never falls on a Friday,* and that this was the first day of that feast is amply shown by the fact that Jesus himself celebrated the Passover the night previous, according to the custom of Jews, who celebrate all their feasts and Sabbaths from eve to eve.

---

*If the first day of Passover falls on Friday, *Hoshanah Rabah*, the seventh day of Booths, would fall on a Saturday, and according to rabbinical law the Jews gather on that day branches of brook-willows for their ceremony, which could not be done on a Sabbath, hence it never comes on a Sabbath; consequently the first day of Passover never occurs on Friday.

Then the scene of the crucifixion tells us that there was not a Jew — at least an intelligent Jew — present; for when Jesus cried, "Eli, eli, lamah Shabaktani?" some of those present thought he was calling Elijah to help him. If there had been a Jew present he would have understood what he said, for it was in pure Hebrew, and that was the popular language, even as it is at the present day among the Jews in Jerusalem, and he would have corrected the misapprehension.

It is thus evident that the Jews neither crucified Christ nor had anything at all to do with it.

Now it is meet to ask, is the Jew of this day, or was he in history past, sanguinary? In other words, are the Jews in general murderers? Is there a tendency or inclination in them to be murderers? The most partial observer must say no; their inclination and tendency seem to be in the opposite direction. There are no murderers among them. Why not? Is it because the law of the land forbids it? The same law ought to hold others in due bounds, but it does not. Why not? Because the Shemitic blood does not run in their veins as it does in the veins of the Jews. Carefully they have kept that blood pure by non-intermarriage with others of doubtful progeny, and the Shemitic blood makes them naturally refined, temperate and law-abiding.

Did not this blood run in their veins just as warm at the time of the crucifixion as it does to-day? Aye, the same blood ran through their veins, and the God-given law that pervades their soul to-day, preserving them from debasing criminality, guided their moral and humane propensities then. The God-given law, wherein their chief seal of life and strength reposes now, ever reposed; and the Jew does not, nor did he ever, delight in shedding human blood.

Why should he have clamored then for the blood of Jesus? He did not.

The Jews did not crucify Christ, neither with their own hands nor were they instrumental in his crucifixion.

THE MESSIAH.

FIRST, the question, what does Messiah mean? naturally presents itself. Messiah, in Hebrew, משיח, means anointed, and is applied in Scriptures to priests, kings, and sometimes to prophets. Aaron and his sons are mentioned as having received the sacerdotal unction; Saul, David, Solomon and other kings the royal unction; and Elisha the prophetic unction. Others may have been anointed of whom Scriptures take no notice, but all that were anointed were chosen to represent what they did, either by God or the people, and the unction was expressive of divine favor of the choice, in consequence of which they were called the messiahs (anointed) of God. In such terms Samuel speaks of Saul (I. Sam. xii. 35), and that appellation is also applied to David (II. Sam. xxiii. 1; Ps. xviii. 51). Even Cyrus, the King of Persia, the friend and benefactor of the Jews, is called God's anointed (Isaiah xliv. 1); while *messiah* in any other term is not mentioned by any other writer in the Scriptures except Daniel, and he speaks so obscurely that it has puzzled commentators for over two thousand years, and to this day none has given a definite explanation of it.

All the prophecies claiming to foretell the coming of a messiah are based only upon constructions, and often upon the merest inference. True, the messianic ideas originated with some rabbis of yore, who, when Israel in exile suffered tyranny and oppression, offered them as a sweet consolation. "Trust in God, O Israel!" were their exhortation. "God will send you a messiah, a deliverer!" But he was never mentioned to be else than a mortal leader — a proclaimer and establisher of that universal peace of which the prophets speak in such glowing terms.

Daniel is the only one who foretells a messiah, and how? In a vision, while immersed in deep prayer, he sees Gabriel and hears him say (Dan. ix. 24), " I am come to show thee — for thou art a favorite — and understand the thing and consider the vision : Seventy weeks are determined upon thy people and upon thy holy city to finish the transgressions and to make an end of sin, and to pardon iniquity and to bring righteousness forever, and to seal up the vision and prophecy, and to anoint the most holy. Know therefore and understand — from the going forth of the decree to return (from Babylon) and to build Jerusalem unto the princely messiah are seven weeks and sixty and two weeks ; the streets shall be built again, and the wall, even in troublous times, and after the sixty and two weeks the messiah shall be cut off, though not for himself; and the people of the coming prince shall destroy the city and the holiness, and the end thereof shall be with a flood, and unto the end of the war desolations are determined. And he shall confirm the covenant with many for one week, and in the midst of the week he shall cause the sacrifice and oblation to cease," etc.

I will not even attempt a detailed commentary on this, as its inaptness to be a prophecy foretelling the Christ of the Christians, or any messiah of such type, is too apparent if viewed uninfluenced by blind faith. Not a particle of this has transpired. The decree went forth from Cyrus to rebuild Jerusalem about three hundred and fifty years before the Nazarene reformer lived, and if the seventy weeks had to be computed into any other time but weeks, why did Gabriel not say so, instead of leaving it to the speculative minds of the various commentators? However, since he failed to do so, and the seventy weeks could not and did not again build up and destroy Jerusalem, it remains as a meaningless dream. Transgression, too, was not punished, sin not ended, and righteousness not come forever, none was anointed, and whatever messiah it alludes to it has failed to verify in this prophecy.

There was to have been a flood and a devastating war, during which the city and holiness were to have been destroyed, and this prince, this messiah, whose name Daniel did not ask, was to have caused the sacrifice and oblation to cease, none of which transpired during the life of Jesus. There was no war, no flood, he was not anointed, and sacrifice and oblation ceased nearly half a century after his death.

Here the question would arise, did the rabbis delude the people by offering them a theory to which there was no foundation? No, they did not. They only gave this great messenger of universal peace the name of messiah, because he was to be one sent by God and accepted by the people, but the foundation of this lies in Scriptures. This rabbinic-messianic era was to be the culmination of time. Scripture defines it as the last of days (Micah iv. 1), when "it shall come to pass that the mountain of the house of the Lord shall be established on the top of the mountains," etc. * * * "And many nations shall say, come and let us go up to the mountain of the Lord, and to the house of the God of Jacob; and he will teach us of his ways, and we will walk in his paths," etc. * * * "Nation shall not lift up sword against nation, neither shall they learn war any more." * * * "For the mouth of the Lord hath spoken it. For all the people will walk each in the name of his God, and we will walk in the name of the Lord our God forevermore."

"Mountain" standing for eminence, it is evident that the religion of Israel — "the mountain of the house of the Lord"— shall stand on that eminence due to it — due to a mother religion. This does not say that any other creed or religion must be abolished, but many nations (as is the case now with enlightened people) shall come and say, "Let us go to the house of the God of Jacob, and he will teach us his ways, and we will walk in his paths," i. e., they will maintain their own religion, but they will begin to adopt the principles of Israel, which are hospitality, charitableness, belief in a common fatherhood of God and brotherhood of man, the result of which is *universal peace;* and after all shall have learned to walk in the paths of the house of Jacob, "nation will not lift up sword against nation any more."

Let us look at the condition of Europe. In any other age, under similar conditions, the swords would have already clashed, the muskets cracked, and the cannons roared, but year by year arbitration is gaining in influence and war averted. There may be terrible wars yet, but the time will surely come when its annihilatory effect will banish war.

It is furthermore evident from the concluding passage that "all the people will walk in the name of their god, and we will walk in the name of the Lord our God forevermore."

In other words, whatever one believes, let him believe it. I will not disturb him, much less hate him or avoid him for it. Let him follow the dictates of his heart and conscience, and I will follow the dictates of my heart and conscience; and both doing so, my neighbor will quote: "Peace on earth, good will to man." And I will quote: "Peace to those who are far and to those who are nigh." And sweet peace will reign supreme. No more shall man hate and oppress man for the love of God. That will be Israel's messianic age.

> "When from pole to pole and from sea to sea
> Men unto man as brother will be;
> When tyrants will cease, and sin no more rage:
> This will be Israel's Messianic age.

> "When from pole to pole and from sea to sea
> One truth will reign, and all creeds will agree;
> When God will be loved by child and by sage:
> This will be Israel's Messianic age."

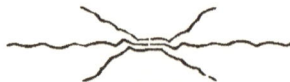

JESUS OF NAZARETH.

WE are often reminded of a prophecy in Scriptures where it foretells that Jesus was to be born in Bethlehem, and yet he is never called Jesus of Beth-lehem, but Jesus of Nazareth. From this it becomes apparent that the prophecy foretelling his birth in Beth-le-hem must have been adopted by modern and not primitive Christian commentators.

Suppose a woman from Chicago would visit St. Louis, and while there give birth to a child, then leave St. Louis as soon as her condition would permit, would that make the child a St. Louisan? Of course not. The same is applicable to Mary, the mother of Jesus. She lived in Nazareth, in the province of Galilee, whence she visited Beth-lehem, where, immediately upon her arrival, she gave birth to a boy; and as soon as her condition allowed she went up to Jerusalem to offer up a sacrifice to God, according as the Jewish law then required, whence she returned home to Galilee (*vide* Luke ii. 4); and her son was called Jesus of Nazareth, not Jesus of Beth-lehem.

The prophecy foretelling his birth in Beth-lehem is claimed to be contained in the following passage: "But thou Beth-lehem Ephrata, though thou be little among the thousands of Judah, yet out of thee shall come forth unto me that is to be ruler in Israel, whose going forth (*have been*) from old, from everlasting." (Micah v. 2.)

We will not stop here, like our Christian interrogator, but continue the chapter. Before doing so, however, we will take the correct translation of the original Hebrew. The words "*have been*," which I have put in parenthesis, are not in the Hebrew version, but were supplied by Christian translators, for what purpose it is not ours to surmise. Then again they mistranslate the words מימי קדם (mimai Kedem) and מימי עולם (mimai olom) as *from old* and *from everlasting*. *Mimai Kedem* is not *from old*, and *mimai olom* is not *from everlasting*, but from *formerly* and from *ancient days* (or this could be from old) would be the correct translation. מעדי עד (me-adai ad) or מעולמי עולמים (me-olmai olonim) would stand for *from everlasting*.

With these errors corrected, we can understand the subject before us more clearly, although we can not see how our interrogator can come to the conclusion as he does even with his translation, when he reads further in the chapter: "And this man shall be the *peace when the Assyrians shall come into our land*," etc.

This person coming out of Beth-lehem, then, shall have been a *man*, no *savior* (of men's souls), no divine being, and he shall have lived at the time when the Assyrians shall have come into the land of Israel, both of which are inapt to ascribe to Jesus.

He is claimed to be a divine being, and surely the prophet should have spoken more understandingly and with more reverence than to simply call him man, and the Assyrian province was merged into Babylonia long before he was born; hence no Assyrians came during his lifetime, and thus he was not the peace above described. Micah spoke here clearly enough of contemporaneous times and events, and it is not necessary to seek in it mystic interpretations. He lived ostensibly during the reigns of Jotham, Ahaz and Hezekiah (see Jer. xxvi. 18 and Micah i. 1), and he knew how often Israel was harassed by the Assyrians during the reckless rules of some kings. When we read then in II. Kings xviii. and II. Chron. xix. that Hezekiah introduced a good reign and withstood the attacks of the Assyrians, uniting eventually the divided Israelites with a grand celebration of the feast of freedom, or Passover (see II. Chron. xxx.), we conclude that the prophet spoke of Hezekiah, who was the son of the wicked Ahaz. The prophet saw his qualities and qualifications, his tendencies and his inclinations, and he understood, and gave utterance thereto, that Hezekiah would be the *man* of *peace*—the man that would subdue Assyria. Just as we of to-day often form opinions of the future of some government after the death of its king, based on our ideas of the crown prince, thus Hezekiah, being the crown prince, the prophet passed on him an encomium, considering him a good regent, which he was as long as he ruled.

The prophet does not say that this man was to be born in Beth-lehem; he only speaks of his descent as a Bethlehemite; and it is a well-known idiom in Scripture language that David is taken as a criterion throughout all its writings. David, the boy of Beth-lehem, was called the father of all the kings of Israel, as also here (see II. Chron. xxix. 2): "And he (Hezekiah) did justly in the eyes of the Lord, according to all, as *his father David* had done."

Let us now return once more to our first passage and test its prophetic contents a little closer: " But thou, Bethlehem Ephrata, though thou be little among the thousands of Judah, yet out of thee shall come forth unto me that is to be ruler in Israel," etc. It bears on its face the mark of inaptitude, in so far that Jesus is not ruler now and never was ruler in Israel. If he rules at all, he rules in

Christendom, with Israel to protest his divine sovereignty and dominion. Thus take the passage as you will, with either of the two translations, that Beth-lehem birth establishes nothing to prove the Christians' claim, and leaves the Jews still of the opinion that Jesus was neither *ruler*, *savior* nor god, but simply Jesus of Nazareth.

WILL GOD PUNISH THE CHILDREN FOR THE SINS OF PARENTS?

JUDAISM is not a religion of chance or speculation, but a religion based on fundamentals that can firmly bear and support the superstructures erected on it. Israel's history bears testimony to this. Judaism, furthermore, fears not the glaring light of the most rigid examination, and dares to stand before the searching gaze of the most critical investigators; and the more it is investigated the better it is understood, hence the better it is understood the better it is appreciated. The older it grows the purer it gets. These remarks I have deemed necessary because some religionists would find scruples to differ with the (so-called) authorized version of the Bible, and would fear to swerve from the adopted ideas of the anteceding Church fathers, priests and rabbis. Formerly there were some who were by some fanatics led to believe that on account of the iniquities of a single sinner a whole congregation or community would be visited by the wrath of God, but this can by no means be substantiated by Scriptural information.

Moses (Deutr. xxiv. 16; Isaiah xxi. 29; Ezekiel xviii. 2) and others clearly expressed that fathers shall *not* suffer for the sins of their children, nor shall children suffer for the sins of their fathers. Would a "*merciful and long-suffering God*" punish one for the sins and wrongs of another? And yet we read in Scriptures, in the very commandments He gave on Sinai: "*I am a jealous God,* who will *visit* the iniquities of the *fathers upon their children,* to the third and fourth generation." (Exod. xx. 5.; Deutr. v. 9.) According to enlightened ideas, this impeaches both the *unity of God* and his *infinite goodness.*

A God who has no equal, hence no rival, of whom should He be jealous? And an *all-good* and *merciful God,* would He punish the innocent for the guilty, even if they were father and son?

To investigate this we must be cognizant of the fact that the writers of the Scriptures made some mistakes in their manuscripts, on account of which the קְרִי (K'ri) and כְּתִיב (K'thib) rule was adopted, i. e., words that are written one way and must be read another way. So, for instance, do we often find written הוּא (hu) he, when it should be read הִיא (hi), she, just the opposite in gender. Likewise does it frequently occur that נַעַר (naar), boy, has to be read נַעֲרָה (naarah), girl. Under this rule we read in Genesis xlix. 11, *iroh* (his foal), while it is written *irah* (her foal), and in the same place we read *sussoh* (his horse), while it is written *sussah* (her horse).

In Exodus iii. 2 we read מַה זֶּה, *mah zeh* (what is this?), while it is written מִזֶּה, *m'zeh* (from this), and so could we cite hundreds of instances from Scriptures which had to be corrected by later translators; as it was, however, not permissible to change the original writing, the letters were left unchanged, but the reading had to be corrected. Is it not, then, possible that the א in קַנָּא (Kanna) should have been

a ה, which would make it קָנֹה (Koneh), like in Jeremiah
l. 11, where a ה stands for an א in דִּשָׁה (dashah)? May this
error not have been left uncorrected by an oversight?

El is power, and not God, although it sometimes stands
for God as a power; but here, where *adonoi elohecho* (the
Lord thy God) precede it — the name of God twice — it is
hardly probable that *el* would stand for God ; but when it
stands for power it would read : " I, the Lord thy God, am
a power, a possessor, visiting the iniquities," etc. "A possessor of heaven and earth." (*Vide* Gen. xiv. 16.)

The word *poked*, from the verb *pakad*, is nowhere employed
in Scriptures to denote punishment; later translators must
have been led astray by Jeremiah's version, where he says
(Jerem. xxxii. 18), "the Lord will give kindness to thousands,
and (מְשַׁלֵּם, meshalem) *recompense* (not visit) the iniquities
of the fathers into the *bosom* of their children ;" but he says
nothing about the third and fourth generations, which
makes the prophet's rendition apparently clear and natural,
without any reference to the subject in question. The
iniquities — the errors — of parents are transmitted by the
laws of nature into the bosom of their children, which the
prophet calls recompensation of the errors of the fathers.

The word *pakad* seems to be a password — a word of
recognition — given to Israel by Joseph in Egypt (see Gen.
l. 24, 25). There he gives the word with the emphasis
characteristic of the Hebrew language as *pakad yifkad* (he
will surely visit). " When Elohim will surely visit you,"
is the passage, " you shall take my bones with you." Did
Joseph mean to say, when God will surely punish you?
We know well that he did not mean that.

When the Lord sent Moses to Pharoah and instructed
him what to say to Israel He gave him the word *pakad* (*vide*

Exod. iii. 16), which seems to have been recognized by that people (*ibid.* iv. 31).

Moses when complying with the request of Joseph to take his bones out of Egypt, *pakad* is mentioned as the reason of his compliance (*vide* Exod. xiii. 19), hence when Israel, less than three months later, stood at the foot of Mount Sinai receiving the commandments, they could hardly have understood *pakad*, unlike in the previous instance, to mean punishment.

Pakad meant to Israel what it expresses in the Hebrew language and in Scripture literature, visitation, i. e., redeeming visitation; and when the infinitely merciful God uttered it in His decalogue it could not have suddenly changed its meaning.

We would, therefore, read the passage like this: " Thou shalt not serve them (the idols), for I, the Lord thy God, am a power, a possessor, who will visit the iniquities of the fathers upon their children, to redeem them from their errors."

This is evidently correct when we consider that in Hebrew the word for punishment is *annash* or *yassar*, and since none of these words is used we can safely say that it was not intended for such. God is too merciful and too benign to punish one for the sins of another, and Scriptures have no passage to assert that He would, but, on the contrary, Moses distinctly says (Deutr. xxiv. 16): " The fathers shall not be put to death for their children, nor the children for their fathers, but each shall be put to death for his own sin."

Jeremiah (xxi. 29) and Ezekiel (xviii. 2) repeat this almost verbatim, and other Scripture writers also promulgate this doctrine.

DOES SCRIPTURE FORETELL ISRAEL'S CONDITION AS IT IS AND EVER WILL BE?

WE notice of late that some Christian commentators of the Bible, in speaking of the lamentable condition of the Jews in Russia, make it appear that the twenty-eighth chapter of Deuteronomy foretells this condition of Israel; and even at that celebrated conference of Jews and Christians held in Chicago this was mentioned. It is thus meet that we should probe this matter and see whether those interpreters are right or not.

The chapter in question foretells, in case of disobedience of the commands and statutes of the Lord, and not because of the rejection of the Messiah, that Israel shall be terribly maltreated, pillaged, robbed, etc., but at the same time it also foretells that they shall be afflicted with such diseases with which Israel is not, and in history past was never afflicted. Quite the contrary, Israel is a healthy race, not even subject to a great many maladies that Christians suffer from. This is a fact acknowledged by life insurance companies and medical authorities. If, then, one part of the chapter is not verified, how can we quote at this remote time the other part as a prophecy now being fulfilled—fulfilled on a people that violate not, but most rigidly adhere to, the laws of God as they conceive them? And that they are honest and sincere in their conviction is evident from the fact that they rather endure all oppressions and persecutions than renounce their faith; and surely they are not suffering for the sins of others, for that would not be in accordance with the mercy of God. I have demonstrated this in the preceding chapter, showing that God would not punish the children for the sins of their parents. How much less would He let an innocent people suffer for the wickedness of others? And surely all Israel are not wicked. There always were and there are now some wicked ones among them, of course, but there are also good and God-fearing men even among the very ones that suffer agonies and torture under the tyrannical persecution of Russia.

If these Bible interpreters so believe in prophecies contained in the Old Testament, why do they not bear in mind, even if it means literally the same, that God will visit the iniquities of the parents upon their children till the *third* and *fourth* generation only (*vide* Exod. xx. 5; Deutr. v. 9), while here it would seem that it extends to infinite time?

The fact is that Deutr. xxviii. was spoken by Moses to Israel living at that time only, and to those that had to pass over Jordan, without any reference whatever to generations thereafter. (See Deutr. xxvii. 2, which is the introductory to the succeeding chapter.)

That this position is correct we perceive from Deutr. xi. 2, where it says: "For I speak not with your children which have not known and have not seen the chastisement of your God, His greatness, His mighty hand, and His outstretched arm," etc. How could this, then, speak to us now at this remote time, if it was not intended for *any* who have not seen the wonders and miracles of God?

Moses, we learn from Scriptures, tirelessly exhorted Israel
to teach their children the ways, statutes and ordinances of
God, but nowhere can we find that children not taught so
should still be held accountable for wrongs they committed
in ignorance, not thinking it wrong?

Christians believe that "through the seed of Abraham,
Isaac and Jacob (vide Gen. xxii. 18; xxvi. 5; xxviii. 14) the
nations and families of the earth (Christians, of course,
included) shall be blessed." Now, in order to fulfill that
which they believe is prophecy, they have persecuted the
object of their blessing — because it was so prophesied —
and they have succeeded in fulfilling parts of Deuteronomy
xxviii. They have scattered them, slaughtered them, made
the "tail and not the head" of them ; they separated parents
from their children; they have done all they could to fulfill
as much as lay in their power of that famous chapter —
because it was the will of God they had to become the instru-
ments ; but when Jesus, by fulfillment (?) of prophecy, was
crucified, the Jews, who, as Christians claim, had crucified
him, had become despised and scorned for becoming God's
instrument.

Why not read that chapter like many other chapters and
passages in Scriptures and acknowledge that you do not
understand it at all, and take the words of Moses (Deutr.
xxix. 29): "Hidden things belong to the Lord our God,
but revealed matters to us and to our children forever? "

If, then, Israel's dispersion and persecution should not
seem to you as natural consequences of the ways and manners during the barbarous, dark and Middle Ages, when
might was right, put it to the hidden things which you can
not fathom, to the mysteries you can not solve, and leave it
to Him who knows all; but to offer me your explanation to

my query why your father, your grandfather and your great-grandfather had abused and mistreated my ancestors and my people, that "*God wanted it so,*" is far from expressing religiousness. Did not God also want — quoting Christianity — " to love those that hate you, to pray for them that despitefully use you," etc.?

What we then want our Christian friends to speculate on now is not why we have suffered, but why we could not live together amicably — now that the refulgent light of civilization beams into every intelligent soul; why we should not bury the past, and clasp each other's hands, and march together onward and forward as brothers of the same human family and children of the same (Heavenly) Father.

DEVIL AND HELL.

WE hear a good deal of talk about devil and hell, and with thundering force are they employed in the pulpits. The New Testament abounds in these expressions, but the Old Testament in the original Hebrew does not contain them.

Moses, the great statesman, leader and teacher, seemed to have no word for them; David and Solomon, the great poets in Psalmody, Proverbialism and Ecclesiastics, do not utter them; and Isaiah, the King of Prophets, with all other prophets and Scripture writers to follow, never taught any doctrines concerning devil and hell.

The word devil, according to Christian Bible translators, is not found once in the Old Testament, except in plural form, and then only four times, and in no other personification than admonishing Israel not to offer sacrifices to him.

The words they render as devil must have been conveyed to the translators either by a tradition known to them only, or it is their own invention, for שְׂעִירִים (s'irim, Lev. xvii. 7 and II. Chron. xi. 15) means goats or hairy ones, probably referring to the goat-god which the Egyptians worshiped, or a "Satyr," in which form the false gods of the heathens were generally represented, but in nowise can it be rendered devil.

Luther, unlike the English translators, renders it "Feld-teufel" (a faun), which is undoubtedly more correct, when we take its translation as the hairy one.

The other word is שֵׁדִים (shaidim, Deutr. xxxii. 17 and Psl. cvi. 37), which means lords or idols, the latter taking its origin probably from the fact that lords — tyrants and despots — often forced the people to deify them, and the Israelites are warned not to offer sacrifice to them, for the Lord He is to be adored, and no other. The word שָׂטָן (satan) would be about the nearest to the translation of devil, but even that means tempter, or hinderer, and אבדון (abadon) is destroyer, but a direct word is nowhere found in the Old Testament, nor in the Hebrew language.

There is likewise no word in the Hebrew for *hell*, and Christian translators have taken the word *sheol* for it, but how incorrect they are is evident from the words of David (II. Sam. xxii. 6). When he said, " The sorrows of *sheol* compassed me about," did he mean hell? Was he in hell alive?

In another place (Ps. cxxxix. 8) he says: " If I make my bed in *sheol* Thou (God) art with me." Is it supposed that God was in hell with David?

Jonah while in the fish prays (Jonah ii. 3): "Out of the belly of *sheol* I have cried unto thee!" Was he simultaneously in hell and in the fish? Can we not see the inapplicability of sheol into hell? The translators themselves depart sometimes from this translation and make it (as in Gen. xxxvii. 35 and other places) grave, and in Job (xvii. 16) it is translated pit; while the late revisers of the Bible knew not better than to leave it sheol, untranslated.

Its correct translation is subterranean cavity, and is used in Scriptures metaphorically, thus when David cries: "Thou wilt not let my soul go down to *sheol*" (not to hell), he prays hopefully to God that He would not permit him to fall into deep despair; and when he moans: "The sorrow of *sheol* compassed me about," he meant to say, "I am almost despondent!"

When he says: "If I make my bed in *sheol* thou art with me," he simply expresses his trust and confidence in God whom he feels that He is with him in his deep despair and grave despondency.

The Jews also were not free from this superstition, but they have learned it from the Heathens, among whom they were forced to sojourn as captives; and Babylon, the cradle of superstition, no doubt, contributed largely to this; yet it was never so universal with them as it was and still is with some other religionists. The Jews, furthermore, are ridding themselves fast of this superstition, cognizant of the sublimity of Judaism, which tolerates no such impure and obscure doctrines.

To treat this etymologically it would seem that hell was made the antithesis to heaven: one to be the abode of the wicked, the other of the just. The abode of the just was then called *Gan-Eden*, garden of Eden, or delights (surnamed Paradise), and the abode of the godless *Gai-Hinnom,* valley of Hinnom; one of transcendant glory and the other of profound ignominy. The one of glory was the place imagined as pleasant and delightful, as the place where the first man and the first woman dwelt while they were yet pure and innocent; and the place of ignominy (surnamed Hell) as gloomy and miserable as the valley of Hinnom (see II. Kings ii. 30; Jerem. xix. 2; ib. xxxii. 35 and II. Chron. xxiii. 6), where children were burned alive as sacrifices to Moloch. Thus the garden of Eden became the place of eternal beatitude, while the fires of the valley of Hinnom—the fires that consumed innocent children— became the everlasting fire of brimstony Gehena.

Religion without *devil, hell* and *paradise* is pure and sublime—it is the religion of love and godliness—a religion issuing from the heart of hearts and not enforced by ordinances and edicts of priests and rabbins.

A religion that prompts us to abstain from evil and wrong because we fear that we will suffer the consequences is false religion, and such abstinence from evil is but animal compliance; nor is the good done with an expectancy of reaping reward truly religious.

To give a hungry person bread worth a penny because God will reward it with a dime's worth of paradise (or heaven), is to enter into a bargain with God speculating on good profit; and then again to abstain from stealing because we fear that we will be sent to hell for it is trying to deceive God, showing Him that we did not steal, although the heart would have desired to do so.

True and enlightened religion is that which prompts us to be and to do good for the love of God and the good itself, and not for the reward that it will bring—not for speculative motives; and to eschew evil should likewise be for the love of God and the abhorrence of the evil.

When we will have reached the summit of enlightenment, and the scintillating spark of true religion—regardless at what shrine it is confessed—will have ignited our soul, we will need no Eden to be held forth as a bribe or inducement to do good, nor will we need the devil and hell to trepidate and keep us from doing evil; but we will do that which is right because the love of God and our fellow-man will be impressed in our heart.

WHICH IS THE TRUE RELIGION?

SOME have an idea that there can be but one true religion and that all others are false; but this idea is just as absurd as to think that there is but one true method of teaching arithmetic or grammar, or that there is but one way to reach London, or that there is but one way to train a child. Some parents train their children differently from others, and yet the same results are reached. Some captains may steer their ship on a different course to reach the same destination as others, but they reach it; and some teachers vary in methods from others, yet their pupils become equally accomplished. Likewise in religion, which has been given to mankind for the government of their morals and virtues. Each creed and each denomination has the same object in view. Each wants to perfect its members in their qualities as good men and women; and, aside of the dogmas that churches contain, they succeed very well, for there are good men and good women in every church and every religion, and that man shall be honest, upright and God-fearing we all agree on. What we do not agree on is matter that pertains to the hereafter—a matter of which none has the remotest knowledge. One believes —and only by faith—that he will reach it by the grace of his Savior, while the other believes that God, the Father, will admit all His children worthy of admittance. And how is the faith transmitted into the bosom? Surely, the Lord would not be so unjust as to imbue one soul with the true religion and the other with the false religion, and then hold the false religionist accountable for his faithlessness. Nay, the Lord would not open the eyes of one and strike the other with opacity. Religion is a matter of education.

The stone-cutter takes the rough ashler and squares it and smoothes it; then polishes it and engraves letters and signs upon it; thus it rests as the cornerstone of a building. That stone will ever bear those letters and signs. Its letters may be filled up with putty or any other substance, but they will be visible. It may be painted over, then some one will take turpentine and wash it off, and there the letters will appear; and except the stone be utterly defaced, the letters and sign engraven on it originally will forever remain there.

Such is the little heart of the babe. Like the rough stone just from the quarries the mother takes it in hand, and with her fondling and caressing smoothes it, then takes the chisel of love and the mallet of affection and engraves into it the insignia of her religion. The lullaby at its cradle is sung with words of the Savior; the first prayer it is taught to lisp is to the Savior; the little stories told to it are of the Savior. The Sunday-school it is sent to is the school where the doctrines of a Savior are taught. The associates and all the surroundings are believers of a Savior, and if that child grows up a religionist it can not be but a believer in the Savior; while with a Jewish child it is just the opposite. Its mother will whisper into its little ears the trust and confidence in a one and indivisible God. It will be taught to pray to God and Him alone, and it will be reared, trained and educated to be a Jew; and with exceptions very rare the Christian lives and dies as a Christian, and the Jew lives and dies as a Jew. And if the Lord would have preferred that the human race should possess one religion, He would not have permitted His prophet to say that "All the people shall walk, each in the name of his god (his religion), and we will walk in the name of the Lord our God" (Micah iv. 5); or, "From the rising of the sun until his going down my name shall be great among the Gentiles" (Mal. i. 11).

This clearly indicates that the cardinal doctrine of religion is the belief of God. All else are ceremonies and customs, adopted at various ages and suitable to the drift of those ages.

To be good, honest, upright, moral and virtuous is suitable and requisite at all ages, and among all nations and peoples. The religion, then, that can accomplish this is a true religion.

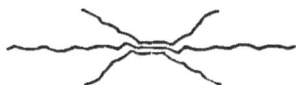